Unlocking The Door to A Stress-Free Home Purchase

Your Educational- Interactive Journal to Home Ownership

Disclaimer: The information provided in this book is for educational and informational purposes only. The author and publisher make no representations or warranties with respect to the accuracy or completeness of the contents of this book and specifically disclaim any implied warranties of merchantability or fitness for a particular purpose. The advice and strategies contained herein may not be suitable for your situation. You should consult with a professional where appropriate. The author shall not be liable for any loss of profit or any other commercial damages, including but not limited to special, incidental, consequential, or other damages.

This Handbook Is Dedicated to My 3 Angels and My Son
Kendrick Lyles Jr.
Everything I do, I do for YOU!

Intro: How I Became a Realtor

As a realtor, I've conducted numerous buyer consultations and taught many first-time homebuyer classes. Each time, I receive glowing feedback on how informative and stress-relieving the sessions are. During one of my buyer consultations, a client remarked, "Mrs. Lyles, you have a lot of great information. Have you ever thought about turning this into a book?" Honestly, I hadn't, but the suggestion made perfect sense, so here we are.

I've always known I wanted a career that allowed me to help others. I have a bachelor's degree in sports medicine and worked as a Home Health Aide while in school. I believe God gave me the perfect heart to be of service to others. One day, after a particularly bad day at work, I realized I no longer wanted to work a 9-5 job. I had a son and was missing out on his childhood, and my husband travels a lot. I was tired of being told when and where I had to be. I wanted to be a great mother and wife.

I called my brother Steve, my go-to person when I'm stressed, and vented about my frustration with my lifestyle. He asked, "Have you ever thought about being a realtor?" I laughed because not only had I never considered it, but I also didn't even understand what a realtor did. Steve said, "With a personality like yours, I believe you would be great at it." I laughed again, but he encouraged me to look up a few realtors on Facebook and follow them for a while.

I took his advice and soon decided I should educate myself more in the profession. Like anyone eager to learn a new skill, I turned to YouTube University. I researched extensively over the next few weeks and created a unique resume—a "promise to be" resume. It essentially stated that if given the opportunity to work and learn from someone, I would do it for free.

I called several brokers, and most said to contact them again once I got my license. I was beginning to feel the sting of repeated rejections when I finally called Broker Debbie Kirkland with

Century21. She was my saving grace. Debbie scheduled an interview with me, and after speaking with her and presenting my "promise to be" resume, she created a position just for me in her office. I became the new ISA for Debbie and her C21 Group.

I learned so much from Debbie Kirkland and her team, and I credit her for my strong work ethic as a realtor today. As her ISA, I was responsible for all follow-up calls, ensuring clients understood the home-buying process, and providing them with the necessary information to start their homeownership journey. Whether it was connecting them with a lender or arranging consultations with other agents in the office, I played a pivotal role in ensuring every client was primed and prepared. The rest is history—I've been rocking and rolling ever since.

Now, I'm excited to share what I've learned from each client over my years as a realtor.

The Emotional Roller Coaster Of Buying A Home?

When you think about purchasing a home, the first thing that may come to mind is, “What’s my credit score?” Then you might ask yourself, “How much money have I saved?” These are valid questions, but they are pretty basic. Have you ever taken a moment to ask yourself if you are emotionally ready to make such a purchase?

Buying a home can be one of the most stressful experiences you can go through. It's a real emotional roller coaster. You're juggling work, saving money, parenting, spousing, hitting the gym, staying hydrated, organizing tons of documents, and answering endless questions—all while trying to keep your day-to-day life on track. It's utterly exhausting! You may not need a therapist, but you absolutely need an emotionally resilient realtor. Someone who can help you stay organized and level-headed throughout the entire journey, ensuring you remain calm and focused.

And this is just scratching the surface. We haven't even delved into what might happen if the underwriter uncovers something unexpected, or if the property doesn’t appraise as expected, or any number of other "what if" scenarios. Just remember, buying a home can be an emotional roller coaster.

Now, let’s talk about what you truly need. When you're in the process of making a purchase and considering what you want in your home, it's essential to think about your future. Here are a few questions to ask yourself:

- Is this your forever home, starter home, or investment property?
- Do you plan on having children?
- Do you plan on staying in the same location long-term?
- Are you buying with a partner? If yes, are you both on the same page regarding your home desires?

- Are you comfortable with your commute to work and your children's school?
- Will you or your spouse need to relocate for your career? If so, will you sell the property or turn it into a rental?

There are many factors to consider when making such a significant purchase. Understanding the answers to these questions can help you create a list of pros and cons for what you're looking for in a property and determine if now is the right time to move. Additionally, it will help you communicate your needs to your realtor. The more you know, the better your experience will be.

The Emotional Roller Coaster of Buying A Home

Questions You Should Answer Before You Start the Process:

1. Will this be your forever home, starter home, or investment property? ________________

2. Do you have children? Do you plan on having more Children? ____________

3. Do you plan on staying in this location long-term? _________

4. Will this be an investment property? ___________

5. Are you buying with your spouse? If yes, are both of you on the same page with what you desire in a home? ___________

6. Does distance matter? How far are you willing to drive from work to home, from school to home? ____________________

7. Is there a probability you will need to relocate for your career? If so, will you sell the property or turn it into a rental?

   ____

8. How soon would you like to move? _____________________

9. What are you looking for in your new home? _____________

   ____
   ____
   ____
   ____
   ____
   ____
   ____
   ____

10. What are your top 3 must haves?

____

____

____

11. Do you require move-in ready or are you willing to do some work? If you are willing to do work, what are you willing to do?

____

____

____

____

____

____

Please take a moment to reflect on the previous questions and jot down your thoughts and concerns. Answering these questions is an excellent first step in clarifying your needs and preferences throughout the process. It also helps your realtor to identify the most suitable properties for you.

You're off to a fantastic start – keep up the great work!

Reviewing Your Funds

Buying a home isn't as simple as strolling into Target and picking out your favorite item (lol). It's also not comparable to purchasing a car, even though cars these days can cost just as much as a home! Buying a home is one of the biggest financial decisions you will ever make and should not be taken lightly. Before you decide to take that step, ensure your finances can handle the impact. Track your spending for at least 30 days to identify where you might be wasting money. After reviewing your bank statements, decide where you can make some adjustments. Do you need to splurge on Starbucks every morning? Consider making your own coffee at least three days a week instead. Monitoring your expenses like this will give you a clearer picture of what you can realistically afford when buying a home.

When I meet with my clients, the questions I ask are: What are you paying for rent right now? Are you comfortable with that payment? Are you comfortable increasing that payment, and if so, by how much? This helps me calculate the mortgage payment for the price range they're considering. One thing you don't want to do is go into debt trying to purchase a property. Once you've decided you're ready to make a move, I hope you've committed to being financially disciplined until you've reached the closing table. This is crucial – we don't want you to have champagne tastes on a beer budget. Yes, you may be pre-qualified for $400K, but do you really want that $400K mortgage payment?

Let's talk about credit scores. In 2024 the ideal credit score to purchase property and utilize all first-time benefits would be a 640 credit score. However, I've helped people purchase homes with a credit score as low as 580. Your credit score plays a significant role in the process but isn't the only determining factor. The most important factor is your debt-to-income ratio. With a 640 credit score, you are eligible for more benefits. As of 2024, here's a breakdown of down payments based on credit scores:

- Under 579 credit score: 10% down
- 580-639 credit score: 3.5% down
- Over 640 credit score: 0% down (depending on available programs)

As you can see, the higher the credit score, the lower the down payment and mortgage. If you don't have a 640 yet but have saved enough cash, you're still in the game. My advice would be to try to hold off until you improve your credit, but you must do what's best for YOU!

Gem Drop: It's crucial to avoid opening any new lines of credit. Keeping your debt-to-income ratio low is key. New hard inquiries can impact your pre-approval amount. So, when you're out shopping and the cashier offers you a store credit card to save 10%, politely decline!

Reviewing Your Funds

1. What are you paying for rent right now? ________________
2. Are you comfortable with that payment? ________________
3. Are you able to increase your payments? If so, by how much?

   ____

What does financial discipline mean to you?

____

____

____

____

What changes are you prepared to make to achieve your goal of homeownership? ________________________________

____

____

____

____

Please list three specific actions you can take to help you save.
Example: I will start by making my own coffee 3 days a week. I will start by the end of the week.

1. I can/will start by

   ____

   ____

2. I can/will start by

   ____

   ____

3. I can/will start by

   ____

   ____

Change is hard, but not harder than you. You Got This!

Having The Money To Support The Dream?

Congratulations! You've made the decision to purchase a home. Are you ready to get started? Yes, we are! (In my cheerleader voice). As we discussed earlier, the higher your credit score, the lower your down payment. Saving for the down payment can take some time if you haven't disciplined yourself for the process. I advise my clients to have at least $5,000 saved, but the most comfortable amount I recommend is $10,000. This is because, while you might have money for the down payment, there are additional out-of-pocket costs associated with purchasing a home. For example, there are closing costs and inspection fees. The bank wants to ensure you have the funds to avoid going into debt when buying a home. The last thing the bank wants to do is foreclose on the property.

When you apply for a home loan, you'll qualify for one of four types of loans: FHA, Conventional, USDA, or VA. I will explain each loan type later. Your loan type will determine your recommended down payment. This is why aiming for a 640 credit score is important. Once you've saved for the down payment, consider the out-of-pocket costs associated with purchasing a property. The timeframe for the out-of-pocket costs varies by state. Here in Florida (Tallahassee), once you go under contract, you will have 3 days to get your earnest money deposit (EMD) to the title company. The EMD is usually 1-2% of the purchase price. For example, if the property is $300K, your earnest money will be $3,000.

Next, there are inspection fees to consider. The inspection includes a full home inspection and a WDO (wood-destroying organism) inspection. These inspections typically cost between $700 and $900 and must be completed within the first 15 days of being under contract. Additionally, there are closing costs to factor in. Although you can ask the seller to cover some of these costs, it's not guaranteed. Being ready for unexpected expenses is essential. After all, do you want to risk losing your dream home over closing costs? Preparation is key to ensuring a smooth homebuying experience.

Gem Drop: I also suggest my clients do two things. First, create a separate account we call the "O NO Account." In this account, start saving a small percentage of each paycheck. This is similar to paying yourself first, just the same as donating a portion of your income for tithes, which are regular contributions made to a church or religious organization. This is important because once you purchase a home, you can no longer call the landlord to fix anything—because YOU are the landlord. Second, use this separate account to live from while you are in the home-buying phase. This is because once you apply for a loan, the lender and underwriter monitor every dime you spend. You must have reserves in the bank before you close. If you have a separate account that you're not using for the home purchase, you can maintain your reserves and still live a little. I'm not suggesting you keep secrets from your lender, but make sure you save properly.

Having The Money To Support The Dream?

Feeling a bit overwhelmed after reading this section? I understand! But don't worry, it's not as scary as it seems. Have you ever wondered why most people buy property between March and June? It's because many receive substantial income tax refunds during this period. Once you decide to take the plunge, it's time to start working on your home-purchasing funds. In the back of this book, you will find a list of out-of-pocket costs along with a list of possible closing costs.

Take a moment to reflect on your thoughts after reading this section.

____

Creating Your Dream Team

Now, it's time to decide what you're looking for in a home. I bet you've already done this part, haven't you? You probably knew the house you wanted before you even made a loan application, browsing Zillow and putting a heart on everything. I know you did because when I meet with my clients for the first time, they usually have several properties they want to send me. I love it! But my question to them is: how much do you think a mortgage on that property would cost, and how much do you have saved for the purchase?

You have to stay on track. Yes, looking for the perfect property is the fun part, but it's even better when you know your price point. So, we'll come back to creating the vision for your dream home once we know what you're working with.

When I teach my classes, the lender and I usually close out the class with one question: Who should you call first, your lender or your realtor? What do you think the right answer is? Well, the truth is, there is no right answer. It doesn't matter who you call first, just make the phone call. Personally, I'd say call the realtor first. Your realtor should have a list of recommended lenders to work with. You'd want to use their lenders because they already have an established relationship and know how to work well together. However, do your part and research lenders as well.

When I meet with clients, I provide them with a list of recommended lenders along with a list of questions to ask. From my personal experience, I've learned that not all lenders are created equal; each one offers different incentives based on your specific situation. That's why I suggest interviewing at least three lenders. This way, you can choose the one that works best with you and for you, ensuring you get the most favorable terms for your home purchase.

When you make the initial loan application, the documents you will need are:

- Driver's license/State ID
- Two months' bank statements
- Two current pay stubs
- Two years of consistent job history supported by tax returns or W-2 forms

Let's discuss a very important topic: Pre-qualification letter vs. Pre-approval letter. When you first make a loan application, answer a few questions, and submit the initial documents, you will receive a pre-qualification letter. It provides an estimate of how much home you can purchase based on the information you gave the lender. Once you complete the loan application and the lender verifies your information, it becomes a pre-approval letter. This letter is a bit more accurate, and that letter is what you will give to your realtor.
Now let's talk about how to find a realtor who works best for you. Just as lenders are not created equal, neither are realtors. With all due respect to my fellow realtors, we all know that some can give the profession a bad name. Finding the right agent is crucial because it will significantly impact the quality of your home-buying experience. The right agent can truly make or break your deal. You need someone who is experienced, reliable, and committed to getting the job done right, ensuring a smooth and successful process from start to finish.

Some might say to find an experienced agent who's been in the business for a while, while others might suggest using your friend's realtor. I say, find someone who matches your personality and style. An experienced agent is great and likely knows their stuff, but they can also be set in their ways and might pressure you into following their route rather than your own. A new agent can be just as good. Think about it: they are hungry, eager to practice what they've learned, and excited to earn their first commission check. Honestly, a new agent might work harder for you than an experienced one.

However, because they are new, they might make small mistakes that could potentially cost you in the long run. But if they have a good broker guiding them, these mistakes can be prevented. In my opinion, the length of time someone has worked in the business is less important than their dedication to their job. Dedication, commitment, and a willingness to go the extra mile will make all the difference in your home-buying experience.

Understanding the roles of a buyer's agent and a seller's agent is crucial. A buyer's agent, as the name suggests, represents you, the buyer. A seller's agent, on the other hand, represents the seller. Can a seller's agent work with the buyer? Yes, depending on the state you're in. I'm often asked if I would recommend a buyer work with the seller's agent, and my answer is that it depends on your situation. Keep in mind that the agent initially represents the seller.
I have been in situations where I represented both the buyer and the seller. In these cases, I was upfront and honest with both parties, showing no favoritism. I disclosed what needed to be shared and represented each client impartially. It was tricky, and I had to be very mindful of my actions.

Gem Drop: When looking for a mortgage lender, it's best to go local. Local lenders are familiar with the regulations and contingencies of the area. They know the agents, understand the local market and are easy to contact. If you need help with the application, you can always drop by their office.

Gem Drop: When applying online, make sure to save all your documents in a file on your computer. Avoid sending pictures of documents to your lender or realtor. Screenshots are difficult to convert into PDF files and can become blurry when enlarged, making it hard to retrieve specific information.

Creating Your Dream Team.

Look up your dream home, and picture yourself making it your own. You have to see it before you can believe it.

1. What are you looking for in a realtor?

   ____
   ____
   ____
   ____

2. What are you looking for in a lender?

   ____
   ____
   ____
   ____

3. Who did you call first your realtor or the lender?

   ____
   ____
   ____
   ____

In the back of this book, you will find a list of questions you should ask your lender and your realtor.

Understanding Your Loan

Alright, you've got all your documents in order, talked to a bunch of lenders, and interviewed a few realtors. Now, it's time to stop stalling and make your move! Understanding your loan type is super important—many first-time buyers overlook this because they're just happy to be approved. But knowing your options can help you stand out in the real estate market. So, let's break down the different loan types:

FHA Loan: A government-backed mortgage insured by the Federal Housing Administration, commonly used by first-time homeowners.

Conventional Loan: These mortgages are not guaranteed by the federal government. They offer low minimum down payments but can be more challenging to qualify for.

USDA Loan: Requires zero money down and is used for purchasing properties in rural areas.

VA Loan: A government-backed loan available exclusively to veterans, service members, and their spouses.

Renovation Loan: This less-discussed loan can be a game-changer. It allows you to purchase a property that needs work, with the cost of renovations included in your loan. I'll explain more about this later. With any loan, you can choose between a fixed rate or an adjustable rate. You'll also need to decide on the term: 30 years (most common), 20 years, or 15 years. Choose what works best for your situation.

Adjustable Rate Mortgage (ARM): Your interest rates fluctuate. It may start with a lower rate, allowing you to afford more property initially, but the rate can increase or decrease over time.

Fixed Rate Mortgage: Your interest rate remains the same throughout the loan term. While it might seem like the obvious choice, an ARM might qualify you for a larger loan, potentially making your dream home more affordable. However, it requires careful budgeting as payments can change. Always keep a reserve fund for unexpected changes.

Just a quick reminder to interview multiple lenders and submit multiple loan applications. Yes, this will impact your credit, but here's a cool trick: if you apply with each lender within 48 hours, it counts as one hard inquiry instead of several. This tells the credit bureau you're just shopping around for the best rate. Also, be sure to compare closing costs, as each lender has its own pros and cons.

I've included a list of questions to ask each lender to help you decide which one is the best fit for you. Once you have your loan amount and pre-approval letter in hand, it's time to create your wish list and start looking at properties. Let's get you into that dream home!

Understanding Your Loan.

This section was full of terms you've probably never heard before. As you were reading this section, which loan type would you prefer?

Take a moment to reflect and write down any questions you may have for your realtor and lender.

You Have Your Pre-Approval Letter! Let's Go Shopping

This is where the excitement begins. With your pre-approval in hand, market research done, and a clear idea of your ideal property, it's time to start viewing homes. This is when dreams turn into reality.

During an initial buyer's consultation, your realtor should ask a lot of questions to understand what you're looking for in a home. I also encourage clients to send me pictures of homes they like if they aren't registered on my website. For registered clients, I can see the homes they're favoriting, which helps me create a personalized list of do's and don'ts.

With your budget and preferences in mind, it's time to start viewing properties! Now, here's an important tip: it shouldn't be our first time seeing the property together. I advise my clients to drive by properties beforehand. Get a feel for the commute to your job, your kids' school, and grocery stores. Try to visit the area at night and during a holiday if possible. This way, you save both time and energy by knowing if a property truly fits your lifestyle before we set up a tour.

When you view properties, take detailed notes—whether the rooms are too small, if there's insufficient closet space, or if the toilet is too close to the sink (yes, it's a real issue). These notes help your realtor refine your home search for a better shopping experience.

This stage can be emotional for clients. Why? Because your mind can play tricks on you, and it's your realtor's job to keep you focused. Do not become a "propertyzilla"—overly picky or unsure, influenced by others' opinions. I advise my clients to take notes and even record walk-throughs if possible, to stay focused, as multiple properties can start to blur together.

Don't feel intimidated if others are also interested in the same property. What's meant for you will find its way to you. Never let anyone pressure you into making a decision. After all, you're the one making the payments and living there, not anyone else. Take your time to ensure you're completely comfortable with your choice. This is a big step, and it's important to make it at your own pace.
I also teach clients about the 80/20 rule I learned from real estate school: There is no such thing as the perfect property. Look for a property with 80% of what you need, 10% of what you can fix later, and 10% of what you can do without. This approach ensures you find a home that meets your essential needs.

Once we find the right property, it's time to make an offer! When you're searching for properties, steer clear of terms like "Pending," "Under Contract," and "Contingent." These indicate that someone has already made an offer, and the property is either awaiting its closing date or still in the contingency period. As a buyer, you might think, "I still want to see it." Honestly, I wouldn't discourage this. Why? Because sellers might accept backup offers. If something goes wrong with the current deal (which is possible), your backup offer could become the next best option, potentially making you the new owner.

As your agent, it's their duty to have your best interests at heart. Some agents may disagree, but consider this: a property listed as "Contingent" today could be "Back on the Market" tomorrow. Without a backup offer, a bidding war could start, which may have been avoided if your realtor called to see if the seller was accepting backup offers. If the seller states they are accepting backup offers, have your realtor submit an offer. This does not mean stop searching for property, by all means, continue with your search until you find the right one. The backup offer assures that if something goes wrong with the first offer, your offer will be next in line.

Before showing you a "Contingent" property, your realtor should call the listing agent to check the contract phase and ensure the sellers are open to backup offers. This avoids giving the buyer false hope.

During your property search, I also encourage looking at For Sale By Owner (FSBO) listings. It's a valuable strategy all realtors and buyers should consider.

If you see a property listed as "Back on the Market" (BOM), don't worry. This doesn't always indicate a problem with the property itself. There are various reasons why a property may return to the market. The previous buyer's financing might have fallen through, or they might have had a change of heart. I often recommend considering BOM properties. It's worth finding out what happened—if the circumstances are understandable it could be a great opportunity to make an offer.

If the listing agent mentions that a buyer backed out due to inspections, don't be overwhelmed. Your realtor can request to see the inspection report and any documentation proving that the issues have been addressed. Additionally, I recommend conducting your own inspections to ensure you're not inheriting someone else's problems.

As a buyer, focus on properties listed as "Active," "Coming Soon," "New," "Back on the Market," and possibly "Price Reduced."

Gem Drop: Once you begin your property search, attending as many open houses as you can is beneficial. It allows you to immerse yourself in the market, get a sense of different neighborhoods, and establish realistic expectations for homes in your budget. Open houses also help you fine-tune your wish list based on firsthand experiences.

You Have Your Pre- Approval, Letter Let's Go Shopping

Just because you're approved for it does not mean you should go for it.

1. What was your pre-approval amount? ____________________
2. What does a mortgage payment look like for that price point? ______________________
3. Are you comfortable with that payment?
   ____
   ____
   ____
4. How many open houses have you attended? ______________
5. Have you created your Do's and Don't List? ______________
   ____
   ____
   ____
   ____
   ____
6. Do you remember the 80/20 rule?
   ____
   ____
   ____
   ____

As you begin viewing properties, as mentioned earlier in this book, it can feel a bit overwhelming. Who do you turn to when your stress levels rise? Name at least 3 people you can call.

Your realtor should be number ONE!

1. ____
2. ____
3. ____

It's Time to Make An Offer!

Stop what you're doing —you've said Yes to the Address! Whether this is your starter home, forever home, or an investment property, you've decided to move forward with the deal. It's time to make an offer.

Before we dive into submitting an offer on your dream home, there's some fun homework to tackle. We'll look into how much similar properties in the area have recently sold for, whether closing costs were covered, and which types of loans were accepted. It might sound like a lot, but this prep work is key to negotiating the best deal for you. I've got your back on the backend stuff so you can stay stress-free and focused on finding your perfect place!
Now that you've made an offer, what comes next? The hardest part – the waiting. You are waiting to see if your offer is accepted, rejected, or countered. What does this mean for you?

If your offer is accepted, you will proceed to the next phase of the contract. If it's rejected, you're back to the drawing board and will continue searching for property.

If your offer is countered, it means the seller does like your offer but has some modifications. They may request you to lower the closing costs you requested, reduce the contingency days, or ask for a higher earnest money deposit. There could be various reasons for a counteroffer.

Rest assured, as a buyer's agent, your realtor will negotiate with the seller's agent to secure the best possible terms for you.

It's Time to Make an Offer!

Take some time and think about what you love about the property.

1. Does it meet all of your requirements?

   ____

   ____

   ____

2. Will it hurt if your offer is not accepted?

   ____

   ____

   ____

3. Are you willing to pay more in Earnest Money to secure your offer? ______________________________________

   ____

   ____

4. Have you researched the neighborhood?

   ____

   ____

   ____

5. Have you driven by the property at night?

   ____

   ____

   ____

6. Does it meet the 80/20 rule?

   ____

   ____

   ____

Before you contact your realtor and say "YES TO THE ADDRESS" make sure you have thought about it and have no regrets! From my experience, you will know when it's time to make an offer.

My Offer Was Accepted, What's Next?

Congratulations! Your offer has been accepted! Get ready to unlock the door to the exciting journey of home ownership.

Where do you go from here?

1. Submit Your Accepted Contract:
    - The first step is to ensure your lender has a copy of the accepted and signed contract. Once they receive it, your loan application will be sent to the underwriter to begin the processing of your loan.

2. Prepare for the Earnest Money Deposit:
    - It's time to write your first check! Depending on your location, you typically have 3 days to deliver your earnest money deposit to the title company.

3. Understand Your 15-day Contingency Period:
    - Now that your contingency period has begun, it's important to know that each state has different regulations. Here in Florida, you have 15 days to complete all inspections and negotiations.

4. Schedule Necessary Inspections:
    - Full Home Inspection: This includes a 4-point inspection and wind mitigation.
    - Wood Destroying Organism Inspection: Essential for checking for termites and other pests.

Whether it's a new construction or a previously owned home, I always, always, always recommend having a full home inspection. Once all inspections are wrapped up and contingencies are cleared, your realtor will give the green light to your lender to order the appraisal. It's smart to hold off on spending more money until this step to avoid any surprises.

Next up, start looking into home insurance options, especially if you're using an FHA loan—they require it before closing. Your loan is now officially in the underwriting stage.

In the meantime, check out the back of this book for a list of what your underwriter is busy with while we wait for the final clearance to close. Keep that excitement going—we're almost there!

My Offer Was Accepted What's Next?

OMG!!! Your offer was accepted, how do you feel?

Take some time and reflect on your journey thus far, are you happy with your realtor and lender?

Are you feeling overwhelmed?

Are you filled with joy and excitement?

Write it down and express your thoughts. What tips will you give a buyer to help them on their journey?

What didn't you like about the process?

What would you have done differently?

____

____

____

____

____

____

The Appraisal, What's that?

Once we wrap up the inspection phase, your loan officer (lender) will step in to order the appraisal. This is to ensure you're not paying more than the property is worth. Remember, the bank will only lend you the appraised value—no extra cash for furniture or renovations (unless you've got a renovation loan).

Now, the appraisal can go a couple of ways. Usually, the home appraises at or above the listed price, giving you instant equity and keeping things moving forward smoothly. But sometimes, it might come in lower than expected. If that happens, the lender will only lend you up to the appraised amount.

If the appraisal comes in lower than expected, don't worry—your contract has protections in place for you. Here's what happens next: The seller has a couple of options. They might ask you to make up the difference in cash, or they could agree to lower the price to match the appraised value if they're still keen to sell.

Occasionally, a seller might choose not to lower the price and opt to wait for another buyer, which was more common in 2019/2020. If this occurs, it can feel like going back to square one, but a well-crafted contract can often prevent this situation altogether. Rest assured, any competent realtor will guide you through this process!

Once you pass the appraisal phase, you're one step closer to crossing the threshold of your new home and can almost celebrate!

The Appraisal, What's That?

Once you receive your appraisal, make sure you review it yourself. If it appraises over the asking price Congratulations, you have instant equity!

1. What did the property appraise for? ____________________

2. Do you have instant equity? If so, how much?

   ____

I Have a Clear To Close!

You've passed the inspection, and both you and the seller agree. So, what's next? You'll likely answer a lot of questions you've already discussed with your lender, resend documents you've already submitted, and verify documents you've previously verified. It may seem repetitive, but it's necessary. Remember, lenders handle multiple files at once, and we all make mistakes. Even I, as a realtor, occasionally forget specific details my clients wanted in their homes. I'm here to get you ready for this journey, ensuring smooth collaboration between lenders, realtors, and clients. We're all in this together. During this phase, it's crucial to avoid spending money or opening new lines of credit. Once you start the process, steer clear of any new credit applications altogether.

Let me share an example: I had a client who was very excited about purchasing a property. We were seven days away from closing when she went furniture shopping and bought a new living room set, dining room set, and bedroom set on credit. This increased her debt-to-income ratio, which affected her loan qualification. How did the lender find out? On the day of closing, all credit and financial information is re-verified. Unfortunately, she didn't close on the expected date.

Another client changed jobs and careers just before closing, which also prevented them from closing on time.

This is crucial. To ensure you get those keys in hand smoothly, we've got to keep things consistent. That means no major changes like switching jobs, opening new lines of credit, quitting your job, or going through any big life changes like divorce.

Stick to these rules until you've officially closed on your home. This consistency ensures you'll get that clearance to close—and bam! You're officially a homeowner. Let's do this!

From The Final Walk-Through to The Closing Table!

You have your clearance to close and are almost ready to get your keys, but there's one last step: the final walk-through. During this phase, you walk through the property to ensure everything is as it was when you first saw it. If the contract included any addendums requiring the seller to perform work or leave specific items (like furniture), this is your opportunity to verify that these conditions have been met. Ideally, you should have already received documentation confirming any required work was done by a licensed professional. During the walk-through, you're just ensuring the property matches your expectations and no drastic changes have occurred.

After completing the final walk-through and you are satisfied, it's safe to say you can schedule the transfer of utilities and complete a change of address form. Within this time frame or a few days prior, you will also receive your closing documents or closing disclosure. This is usually 1-3 days before closing. Your closing disclosure provides a detailed review of your loan agreement, including the loan amount, a breakdown of your monthly payments, and closing costs. It should match what you saw on your loan estimate.

Once you have reviewed and signed all documents, you and your realtor will meet at the title company to sign additional paperwork, potentially meet the seller, and finally receive the keys to your new HOME!

Congratulations, you did it! You've prepared mentally, spiritually, emotionally, and most importantly, financially to become a stress-free homeowner! I bet you're feeling excited, motivated, and ready to embark on this journey to financial freedom. I'm thrilled for you. Just remember, having an agent and lender who truly works for you and with you is the key to making this dream a reality.

From The Final Walk-Through to The Closing Table!

Congratulations you are a homeowner! Make sure you do not forget:

1. Transfer all utilities
2. Complete a change of address form
3. Find out what day is trash day
4. Change the locks
5. Install your security Cameras

This section of the book includes various thoughts and ideas that I believe can offer you a new perspective. Take a moment to envision the possibilities that open up when you think outside the box. What if we start educating not only ourselves but our children at an early age about home ownership, and how to be prepared to embrace financial freedom? Let's unlock the doors to a different mindset.

The Shift: Thinking Different.

According to the Homeownership Data in Zillow's housing trends, the average age for homeownership in 2024 is 41. Can you believe that? Well, with the rising costs of gas, food, and other essentials, it does make sense. But what if we started educating not only ourselves but also our children about homeownership?

I've included a game board that you and your children can use to follow and keep track of each phase of the homeownership journey. This tool can help educate your children, nieces, nephews, siblings, or anyone you want to see succeed in this game of life. Remember, you don't have to purchase your FOREVER home (or as I like to say, your GRAVESTONE) right away. Start with a starter home, or as I call it, a Steppingstone. The idea that you only buy one house in your lifetime is outdated. Owning multiple properties is the new path to early retirement.

Consider this: if you have a student graduating from high school and heading to college, would you prefer to A) pay dormitory fees, or B) purchase a small townhome, add your student's name to the deed, and have them choose roommates who pay rent? This rent can cover the mortgage and taxes, allowing your student to live rent- and debt-free. If your student has worked throughout high school and saved money, and you've helped boost their credit score by adding them to your credit card, they could be ready to purchase their first property after their freshman year. Once they've graduated, they could sell the property and use the proceeds to buy another or keep it as an investment property and rent it out. If possible, rent out the first property, and purchase another, starting a real estate portfolio at a young age.

Do you see where I'm heading with this? As parents (if you have children), it's important to consider our future as we age. We want to ensure we're not relying on our children for support. Homeownership can offer security as you grow older. When you retire and may no longer be working, owning a home allows you to sell and downsize to a retirement community or even build a mother-in-law suite on your children's property with the proceeds from the sale. Have you thought about buying land and a tiny home? The possibilities are endless!

Owning a home is the American dream for many reasons, with the most important being financial security. Let’s ensure we are educating ourselves and others about the benefits of homeownership.

Land Vs Property

As a realtor, I am often asked whether one should buy land or property. My response is: What is your goal? This question can be answered in various ways depending on your objectives.

If you're considering building in the future and spot a chance to buy land in your preferred location, don't hesitate to make the purchase. Even if your dream home isn't within reach yet, investing in a piece of land in a desirable or emerging area can be a smart move. Why? Because you can sell the land down the road and use the proceeds to buy a property that suits your needs. It's a strategic way to secure your future in real estate.

Given the property shortage we are experiencing in 2024, land can be incredibly valuable. Why? Because you need land to build. Whether it’s for a new store, a new community, or someone looking to build their dream property, land is essential.

The key to land investment is location, location, location.

Buyer's Representation Agreement, What Is That?

A buyer's representation agreement is like a partnership contract between you and your realtor. Is it legally binding? No, but it does give your agent the green light to work exclusively with you. This means they can focus fully on your home search without competing with other realtors.

Here's the deal: we realtors don't get paid until you find your dream home. Imagine if we've spent time sharing property info, showing you multiple homes, and giving you top-notch real estate advice—then another agent swoops in to seal the deal and takes credit for all our hard work. Signing a buyer's representation agreement ensures everyone's on the same page and protects the relationship.

This is why it's crucial to choose an agent you like and trust to have your best interests at heart.

In real estate school, we heard a story about an agent who invested in showing properties to her clients. One day, her clients attended an open house, fell in love with the property, and made an offer with the hosting agent. They thought their original agent would still get the commission, but she didn't because there was no signed agreement between them.

The moral of the story is to be committed to your agent.

"We're Not Married, But We Plan to Be"

As a realtor, I always advise my clients during buyer consultations to bring along anyone involved in their decision-making process. I emphasize this for multiple reasons, but primarily to avoid being pulled in multiple directions. When clients bring their boyfriends/girlfriends or fiancés, I often have difficult conversations with them—conversations they might not want to hear.

As a realtor, it's important to discuss hypothetical situations that may arise: What if you break up? What if one partner leaves and doesn't return? It's crucial to understand that once you purchase property together, selling it requires both parties' agreement. Breakups often bring challenges, especially when it comes to shared property, which can lead to complex and emotionally charged situations.

Before making such a significant commitment, it's crucial to understand each other's pasts. Here's a true story: A young lady asked me to represent her and her boyfriend in purchasing a property. I had my talk with them, and despite my warnings, they decided to proceed. Fifty-five days later, they closed on the property. Four years passed, and I received a call from her saying she wanted to sell. During our seller's consultation, we discovered two major issues: she hadn't heard from him in a year, and there was a lien on the property due to his back child support from a previous relationship. This meant she couldn't sell the property without his cooperation, or without paying the back child support to remove the lien.

Had she listened to my advice, they could have avoided this situation. I suggested they both purchase separate properties, as they had the credit and funds to do so. They could have lived in each other's homes occasionally to get a feel for paying a mortgage. After two years, one could sell or turn the property into an investment, and then they could move in together. This strategy would have given them financial flexibility and stability.

The key takeaway here is to make wise, long-term decisions. While everyone hopes for a lasting partnership, it's essential to plan realistically. By making informed choices, you can safeguard yourself against potential complications down the road.

The Best Way to Stay Current in Today's Market

The best way to stay current in the market is to attend as many open houses as possible. It may sound crazy, but it's true. Doing so keeps you updated on prices and locations and helps you create a wish list for your property, giving you ideas of what you may want to implement in your new home.

If you have a specific location in mind, focus on attending open houses in that area. It's perfectly fine to be curious and visit all the open houses you can. Once you're actively in the market, make it a regular Saturday activity. You might be surprised by what you find.

When Should I Make a Loan Application?

When is the right time to make a loan application? Now! Even if you're not quite ready to move forward, it's wise to know where you stand. Think of it this way: if the end goal is homeownership, you need to know your starting point to reach that finish line.

I often hear people say they checked their credit score on Credit Karma, but for a mortgage loan, that's not accurate. Lenders evaluate all three credit scores and use the median score to determine your loan eligibility. It might seem depressing, but it's better to identify areas for improvement beforehand than to fall in love with a home you can't buy because you did not qualify for the loan.

Worried about how it affects your credit? Yes, it does result in a hard inquiry, but understanding where you stand and what improvements are needed is crucial. The bottom line? Start the loan application process now, even if you're not quite ready to proceed. It's all about getting prepared.

Marry The House Date the Rate: What Does That Mean?

This could be the year of opportunity for you. While interest rates may concern you, remember that no one wants to pay high interest rates. Waiting for the perfect rate may cause you to miss your opportunity to make a move. Seize the moment to potentially obtain your dream home at the right price.

Waiting for rates to drop carries risks. When rates decrease, there's typically a surge in buyers, which shrinks inventory and ramps up competition, potentially driving prices higher. Seize the current market opportunity to position yourself for success. Don't wait for ideal conditions—take action now. It's all about "marrying the house and dating the rate."

Rates may not be in your favor at the moment, but you've just found your dream house. Yes, you can afford it, but you don't like the current rate. Did you know that once rates drop, you can refinance your property to a lower rate? For example, if you purchased a property in 1991 when rates were 9.25%, and in 1998 rates dropped to 6.94%, you could call your lender or mortgage company and refinance to the current rate.

Benefits of Refinancing:

- **Lower Monthly Payments**: A reduced interest rate typically results in lower monthly mortgage payments.
- **Interest Savings**: You pay less in interest over the life of the loan.
- **Debt Consolidation**: Refinancing might allow you to consolidate other high-interest debts into your mortgage.
- **Change Loan Terms**: Adjust the loan term to pay off your mortgage faster or extend it for smaller payments.

What to Consider:

- **Closing Costs**: These can be substantial and should be weighed against potential savings.
- **Break-Even Point**: Calculate how long it will take to recoup the costs of refinancing through the savings on your monthly payments.
- **Equity**: Ensure you have sufficient equity in your home to qualify for refinancing.

Take advantage of the current market conditions and position yourself for future success. Don't wait for the perfect moment—make your move now.

The Property Appraisal Said…

This is my favorite section. The reason is because I hear all too often, "The property appraisal site said the property is only worth XYZ." Now, it's good to do your own research on a property, but you need to know what you are researching. When you look at the property appraisal page, you should check if the taxes have been paid, if the property is in a flood zone, and if any work done on the property has been properly permitted.

Additionally, these sites provide valuable neighborhood information like school zones and historical data on the property. However, it's important to note that these sites do not give you the true value of the property—only the land value. This is why your mortgage lender orders an appraisal to get the true value of the home.

When it comes to accurate valuation, especially for significant transactions, engaging a professional appraiser is essential. They provide detailed and precise assessments based on thorough inspections and current market conditions. While using appraisal websites can offer initial insights, it's imperative to supplement their estimates with professional appraiser guidance for important real estate decisions.

So, yes, it's good to review the property appraisal site, but always listen to your realtor.

Last Minute Thoughts:

- Make sure you shop around constantly for home insurance. As your home value increases, so will your taxes and insurance payments.

- Make additional payments on your mortgage whenever possible. Doing so can transform a 30-year loan into a 25-year loan or even less. Since the interest is front-loaded and based on the loan balance, reducing that balance quickly means you'll make fewer payments and pay less interest overall. Even one extra payment a month can significantly benefit you.

- Don't end your relationship with your realtor after the transaction. You've spent 30 days in constant communication, but getting your keys doesn't mean it's over! As a realtor, I want to be your ongoing resource for all things real estate. Need a painter, plumber, or any other service? Reach out to your realtor.

- Keep all of your closing documents together and in a safe place. If possible laminate it.

- **Do not forget to file your homestead exemption.**

- Do not deposit large sums of money into your bank account without proper explanation. Even a gift fund would have to be verified. (I started to make this a section of the book)

- Do not dispute items on your credit while in the process of underwriting.

- Your approval letter proves that you have what it takes. Don't let fear prevent you from seizing your blessing.

- Do not change your financial status during the process. Example: No new jobs, no new lines of credit, and do not divorce your spouse while you are in the process of making a purchase.

- Keep in mind it can be stressful but it’s all worth it in the end

Out Of Pocket Cost

As we embark on the exciting journey of purchasing your dream property, it's crucial to be aware of the potential **Out-Of-Pocket Expenses** associated with the process. Understanding these costs will help us plan effectively and ensure a smooth transaction.

- Earnest Money Deposit:
  - Typically ranges from 1% to 3% of the home's purchase price.
  - This deposit demonstrates your serious intent to purchase the property.

- Home Inspection Fees:
  - Varies based on the size and location of the property.
  - An essential step to identify any potential issues before finalizing the purchase.

- Appraisal Costs:
  - Generally, falls in the range of $300 to $500.
  - Ensures that the property's appraised value aligns with the agreed-upon purchase price.

- Closing Costs:
  - Typically 2% to 5% of the home's purchase price.
  - Includes various fees such as title insurance, attorney fees, and document preparation.

- Loan Origination Fees:
  - Usually around 0.5% to 1% of the loan amount.
  - Covers the administrative costs associated with processing your mortgage.

- Escrow Fees:
  - Varies but is often split between the buyer and seller.
  - Facilitates a smooth and secure transaction process.

- Homeowner's Insurance:
    - The cost depends on the property's location and coverage.
    - Essential for protecting your investment against unforeseen circumstances.
- Property Taxes:
    - Calculated based on the property's assessed value and local tax rates.
    - Paid either at closing or as part of your monthly mortgage payments.
- Home Warranty:
    - Optional but recommended for added protection against potential repairs.
    - Typically costs around $300 to $600.
- Utilities and Maintenance:
    - Initial setup fees for utilities and potential maintenance costs.

It's essential to note that these figures are estimates, and actual costs may vary.

Questions You Should Ask Your Lender

When guiding first-time homebuyers through the mortgage process, it's crucial for them to ask the right questions. Here are some key inquiries for a mortgage lender:

- **What types of loans do you offer?**
    - Understanding the various loan options helps you choose the one that best suits your needs.
    -
- **What is the interest rate, and how is it determined?**
    - Knowing the interest rate and the factors influencing it is vital for long-term financial planning.
    -
- **What are the closing costs?**
    - You should have a clear picture of all the fees involved in the closing process.
    -
- **What is the down payment requirement?**
    - Understanding the down payment helps you prepare financially for this upfront cost.
    -
- **Are there any prepayment penalties?**
    - Knowing if there are penalties for paying off the mortgage early is important for those planning to do so.
- **What documents are needed for pre-approval?**
    - Having the necessary documentation ready streamlines the pre-approval process.
- **How long does the mortgage approval process take?**
    - Knowing the timeline helps you plan your home search and purchase accordingly.

- **What is the difference between pre-qualification and pre-approval?**
  - Clarifying these terms ensures that you understand the level of commitment from the lender.

- **Are there any special programs for first-time buyers?**
  - Some lenders offer specific programs or incentives for first-time homebuyers.

- **What is the maximum loan amount I qualify for?**
  - Understanding the loan limit helps you focus on homes within your budget.

I encourage you to ask these questions. It will not only empower you in the home-buying process but also establish a transparent and communicative relationship with the mortgage lender.

What Does the Underwriter Do?

A loan underwriter plays a crucial role in the mortgage loan approval process by evaluating the risk of lending money to a borrower. Here's a breakdown of what a loan underwriter does to get a mortgage loan approved:

1. **Reviewing Documentation**:
   - **Income Verification**: The underwriter reviews the borrower's income documents, such as pay stubs, tax returns, and employment verification, to ensure the borrower has a stable and sufficient income to repay the loan.
   - **Credit History**: They analyze the borrower's credit report to assess their creditworthiness, including credit scores, payment history, and outstanding debts.
   - **Assets**: The underwriter examines bank statements, investment accounts, and other asset documentation to verify the borrower has sufficient funds for the down payment, closing costs, and reserves.

2. **Evaluating Debt-to-Income Ratio (DTI)**:
   - The underwriter calculates the borrower's DTI ratio to ensure it falls within acceptable limits. This ratio compares the borrower's monthly debt payments to their monthly gross income to determine if they can manage the additional mortgage payment.

3. **Assessing Property Appraisal**:
   - The underwriter reviews the property appraisal report to ensure the home's value supports the loan amount. This helps determine that the property is worth the purchase price and can serve as sufficient collateral for the loan.

4. **Checking Employment Stability**:
   - They verify the borrower's employment history and stability to ensure ongoing income. This may include

contacting the employer for confirmation or checking the length of time the borrower has been employed in their current job.

5. **Ensuring Compliance with Loan Guidelines**:
    - The underwriter ensures that the loan application complies with the specific guidelines of the loan program (e.g., FHA, VA, conventional loans). This includes verifying that all required documentation is complete and accurate.

6. **Assessing Borrower's Financial Behavior**:
    - They look for red flags such as large, unexplained deposits, recent significant purchases, or any other financial behavior that might indicate potential risk.

7. **Risk Assessment**:
    - Using all the gathered information, the underwriter evaluates the overall risk of lending to the borrower. They consider factors like loan-to-value ratio (LTV), DTI, credit score, and financial stability.

8. **Decision Making**:
    - Based on the assessment, the underwriter can:
        - **Approve the loan**: If the borrower meets all the criteria.
        - **Approve with conditions**: If minor issues need to be addressed or additional documentation is required.
        - **Deny the loan**: If the borrower does not meet the required guidelines or poses too high a risk.

9. **Communicating with the Loan Officer**:
    - The underwriter communicates their decision to the loan officer, who then informs the borrower. If there are conditions to be met, the loan officer helps the borrower address them.

By thoroughly assessing the borrower’s financial situation and the property's value, the loan underwriter ensures that the mortgage loan is a sound investment for the lender.

HELPFUL STRATEGIES

- Save all pay stubs, and bank documents.
- Keep copies of all documents submitted for processing.
- Continue to pay all debts and loans on time.

COMMON MISTAKES MADE

- No cash deposits
- No large purchases on your credit card
- Do not apply for any type of new credit. ie..Dillards, Target, Victoria. Secret, ect
- Do not change bank accounts.

REMEMBER

Once the transaction is over that does not mean my job is done. I want to be a resource for all your real estate needs. I have plenty of recommended vendors that could help with light to total renovations. Save my contact information!

Thank You!

Thank you for entrusting me, Erica Lyles, your favorite realtor, to lead you through the home-buying process. I hope you feel empowered, well-informed, and prepared to take the next step in your journey toward homeownership. This journey was crafted specifically with you in mind!

I want to ensure you are well-informed as you and your realtor navigate these real estate streets.

Tips From A Few Of My Clients:

You can change every single thing about a house, even knocking it down and rebuilding, but you can not change location -- **Mrs. Foss**

Keep your credit on point, that's your lifeline. It is very important. Keep your debt-to-income ratio low, if you have a lot of debt it looks as if you can not afford the home. Even though you feel you can -- **Mrs. Smith**

Be patient and do not allow fear to push you away from your dream. Trust the process and trust your gut feeling -- **Mrs. Daniels**

Trust your agent and make sure you get a good home inspection -- **Mr. Falcom**

Made in the USA
Middletown, DE
29 July 2024